HAKIM SANAI:

THE WALLED GARDEN
OF TRUTH

Translated and abridged
by

DAVID PENDLEBURY

THE OCTAGON PRESS
LONDON

Copyright© 1974 by David Pendlebury

ISBN 900860 35 9

First impression in this Edition 1974
Second impression 1984
Third impression 1989

Printed and bound in Great Britain at
The Camelot Press Ltd., Southampton.

CONTENTS

Foreword   5

Biographical Note   7

'The Garden of Reality' (*The Walled Garden of Truth*)   9

Afterword   53

Reading List   75

FOREWORD

The following pages have been assembled from notes which I made in the course of studying Major J. Stephenson's edition of Hakim Sanai's classic.* Since this present work could not have been undertaken without the aid of Stephenson's book, it is only proper that I should register my indebtedness to this scholar at the outset. If at times, in my subsequent discussion of the text, I appear critical of his particular approach to the task, this should not be allowed to obscure the gratitude and admiration he deserves for having taken a first step towards making Hakim Sanai's writings available to the English-speaking public.

The aim has been to take the process a step further by putting a selection of Sanai's thoughts into readable modern English, and offering it to the growing number of informed readers from all walks of life who are beginning to discover the relevance of certain traditional Middle-Eastern ideas to contemporary preoccupations in the West.

*The first book of the Hadiqatu'l-Haqiqat, edited and translated by Major J. Stephenson, Calcutta 1910.

This cutting and polishing process has not taken place entirely in a vacuum of arbitrary personal whim. We are fortunate today, in a way that Major Stephenson and other eminent western scholars have regrettably not been in the past, in having available first-hand guidance in the interpretation of the spirit, as opposed to the letter, of classical Sufi materials. I have in mind the work of Idries Shah, and others like him, who have effectively freed the study of Sufism from the distressingly irrational restrictions and distortions to which it has been subjected. Sufi studies have been lifted out of the academic arena altogether, and placed fairly and squarely where they belong—within the reach of ordinary people. Such a process of popularization is the very reverse of a dilution or degradation of the source materials: it is an indication of a trend whereby a vital teaching is no longer being held at arm's length but is now being allowed to weave itself, in a most timely way, into the fabric of our culture. In this present undertaking, Shah's work has served both as an encouragement and a touchstone.*

*This is not to say that this development is unwelcome in the academic world: only that the emphasis has changed. In *Sufi Studies East and West* (E. P. Dutton, New York, 1973 and Jonathan Cape Ltd., London, 1974) twenty-four international scholars, including many Orientalists and specialists in Sufi thought and literature, have contributed papers analysing and welcoming the development. In a further area—psychology—over two hundred universities and colleges have adopted Professor Robert Ornstein's *The Psychology of Consciousness* (W. H. Freeman and Viking, 1972) which equates Shah's writings with contemporary discoveries in brain-function.

Biographical Note

What little information there is concerning the life of Hakim Sanai probably has more mythical than historical validity. He flourished during the reign of Bahramshah (1118—1152) and probably died in 1150. Apparently he was already a poet of some eminence at the court at Ghazna, when he underwent a crisis of identity. In his 'Memoirs of the Poets', Sirajuddin Ali gives the following anecdote.

Sanai had just written a poem in praise of Sultan Ibrahim of Ghazna, and was on his way to deliver it at the court before the monarch set out on another punitive expedition to India. The sound of singing coming from a garden caught his attention, and he stopped to listen. It was Lai-Khur, a notorious drinker and 'madman', whose outrageous utterances frequently contained more than a grain of truth.

Lai-Khur called for wine and proposed a toast 'to the blindness of Sultan Ibrahim'. When objections were raised, he insisted that the Sultan deserved blindness for embarking on such a mad escapade when his presence was needed at home.

Then a toast was called 'to the blindness of Hakim Sanai'—which must have given the eavesdropping poet a considerable jolt. There were even stronger objections to this on the grounds of Sanai's excellent reputation. But Lai-Khur countered that the toast was even more apt, since Sanai seemed unaware of the purpose for which he had been created; and when he was shortly brought before his Maker, and asked what he had to show for himself, he would only be able to produce eulogies of kings—mere mortals like himself.

The narrator goes on to say that the impact of these words caused Hakim Sanai to seek instruction from the Sufi Master, Yusuf Hamadani.

It is also related that Bahram Shah offered to make him his brother-in-law; but Sanai graciously turned down the offer and set out forthwith on a pilgrimage to Mecca. On his return he began writing the *Hadiqat*, which he completed some time after 1130 A.D.

THE GARDEN OF REALITY
(extracts)

The seeing soul perceives
the folly of praising
other than the creator.

The self is a servant in his cavalcade;
reason a new boy in his school.
What is reason in this guesthouse,
but a crooked scrawling
of God's handwriting?

Had he not shown himself,
how should we have known him?
Unless he shows us the way,
how can we know him?

We tried reasoning
our way to him:
it didn't work;
but the moment we gave up,
no obstacle remained.

He introduced himself to us
out of kindness: how else
could we have known him?
Reason took us as far as the door;
but it was his presence that let us in.

But how will you ever know him,
as long as you are unable
to know yourself?

Once one is one,
no more, no less:
error begins with duality;
unity knows no error.

Place itself has no place:
how could there be place
for the creator of place,
heaven for the maker of heaven?

He said:
'I was a hidden treasure;
creation was created
so that you might know me.'

Why, tell me, if what you seek
does not exist in any place,
do you propose to travel there on foot?
The road your self must journey on
lies in polishing the mirror of your heart.

It is not by rebellion and discord
that the heart's mirror is polished free
of the rust of hypocrisy and unbelief:
your mirror is polished by your certitude,
—by the unalloyed purity of your faith.

If you want the mirror to reflect the face,
hold it straight and keep it polished bright;
although the sun does not begrudge its light,
when seen in a mist it only looks like glass;
and creatures comelier than angels even
seem in a dagger to have devils' faces.

Your dagger will never tell you true from false:
it will never serve you as a mirror.
Better to seek your image in your heart
than in your mortal clay, break free
from the chains you have forged about yourself;
for you will be free when you are free of clay.
The body is dark—the heart is shining bright;
the body is mere compost—the heart a blooming
        garden.

Don't sew up the bag,
or tear at the veil;
don't lick that man's plate,
or buy his flattery.

He doesn't know his own self:
how should he know the self of another?

He knows only his hands and feet,
how should he know about God?
This is beyond the sage's grasp:
you must be a fool
if you think that you know it.
When you can expound on this,
you will know the pure essence of faith;
till then,
what have faith and you in common?
It is better to be silent
than to talk nonsense
like one of the learned;
faith is not woven
into every garment.

You were made for work:
a robe of honour awaits you.
How is it that you are satisfied
with mere rags?
How will you ever have riches
if you are idle sixty days a month?

Knowing what you know,
be serene also, like a mountain;
and do not be distressed by misfortune.
Knowledge without serenity
is an unlit candle;
together they are honey-comb;
honey without wax is a noble thing;
wax without honey is only fit for burning.

Leave this abode
of birth and decay;
leave this pit,
and make for your destined home.
This heap of dust is a mirage,
where fire seems like water.

The pure man unites
two in one;
the lover unites
three in one.

But I am frightened
lest your ignorance and stupidity
leave you stranded on the bridge.

He is the provider
of both faith and wordly goods;
he is none other
than the disposer
of our lives.
He is no tyrant:
for everything he takes,
he gives back seventy-fold;
and if he closes one door
he opens ten others to you.

You cannot distinguish
the good from the bad.
He treasures you more
than you do yourself.

That friend of yours is a serpent:
why do you knock at his door?
That serpent is your friend:
why do you run from him?

Rise, said Mansur,
have done with fairy-tales;
leave your base passions,
and come to me.

You have to realize
that it is his guidance
that keeps you on the path,
and not your own strength.

Through him* the leprous body became whole,
and the sightless eye became bright.
Anyone who, like him,
seeks neither name nor fame,
can produce ten foods from one jar,
can make a stone as fragrant as musk,
can bring the dead to living action and speech,
can breathe life into the dead earth of the heart.

How shall this sluggish body worship him?
How shall he be known to life and soul?
A ruby, there, is just a piece of stone:
and spiritual excellence the height of folly.
Silence is praise—have done with speech;
your chatter will only bring you harm and sorrow;
—have done!

*Jesus.

14

Belief and unbelief
both have their origin
in your hypocrite's heart;
the way is only long
because you delay to start on it:
one single step
would bring you to him:
become a slave,
and you will be a king.

The dumb find tongues,
when the scent of life reaches them
from his soul.

Listen truly—and don't be fooled—
this is not for fools:
all these different shades
become one colour
in the jar of unity;
the rope becomes slender
when reduced to a single strand.

Your intellect is just a hotch-potch
of guesswork and thought,
limping over the face of the earth;
wherever they are, he is not;
they are contained within his creation.
Man and his reason are just the latest
ripening plants in his garden.
Whatever you assert about his nature,
you are bound to be out of your depth,
like a blind man trying to describe

the appearance of his own mother.
While reason is still tracking down the secret,
you end your quest on the open field of love.

The path consists in neither words nor deeds:
only desolation can come from these,
and never any lasting edifice.
Sweetness and life are the words
of the man who treads this road in silence;
when he speaks it is not from ignorance,
and when he is silent it is not from sloth.

These learned fools, these thieves and pickpockets:
they use what they have learnt for highway robbery!
Listen to me, you lord of language:
better fill your heart with light,
than with a hundred thousand words;
when silent you are eloquence itself:
open your mouth, and you're a rabble-rouser.

Nobody sees the heart and soul
of the seeker after truth;
but his tongue speaks truly:
'I am the truth.'

For the wise man
evil and good
are both exceeding good.
No evil ever comes from God;
whenever you think to see
evil proceeding from him,

you were better to look on it
as good.
I'm afraid that on the way of faith,
you are like a squinter seeing double,
or a fool quarrelling with the shape of a camel.
Evil can never arise from him:
how should evil co-exist with him?
Only the foolish and ignorant work evil,
—never the beneficient friend.
If he gives you poison, deem it honey;
and if he shows you anger, deem it mercy.

Have you never seen how a nurse,
in the earliest days of an infant's life,
one minutes leaves it crying in the cot,
and holds it to her breast the next;
sometimes smacks it, sometimes soothes it;
now drives it away, now makes a fuss of it?
A stranger seeing this is angry:
'She doesn't care about the child' he sighs.
How could he know that the nurse is right,
and that this is the way she has to work?

Be contented with your lot;
but if you have any complaints,
go and take them to the Cadi,*
and obtain satisfaction from him.
—That's how the fool's mind works!

Whatever befalls you,

*Cadi: Judge.

misfortune or fortune,
is unalloyed blessing;
the attendant evil
a fleeting shadow.
How should the author
of 'Be, and it was.'
ever bring down evil
on his own creation?
'Good' and 'evil' have no meaning
in the world of the Word:
they are mere names, coined
in the world of 'me' and 'you';
in God's creation there is no such thing
as absolute evil.

Your life is just a morsel in his mouth;
his feast is both a wedding and a wake.
Why should darkness grieve the heart?
—for night is pregnant with new day.

You say you've unrolled the carpet of time,
and passed beyond the four, beyond the nine:
step then beyond life itself and reason,
till you arrive at God's command.

You cannot see anything, being blind by night,
and by day one-eyed with your foolish wisdom!

Humility suits you, violence doesn't:
a naked man frantic in a beehive
is out of place.

My friend, everything existing
exists through him;
your own existence is a mere pretence.
No more nonsense! Lose yourself,
and the hell of your heart becomes a heaven.
Lose yourself, and anything can be accomplished.
Your selfishness is an untrained colt.

Your are what you are:
hence your loves and hates;
you are what you are:
hence faith and unbelief.

Hope and fear drive fortune from your door;
lose yourself, and they will be no more.

At his door, what is the difference
between Moslem and Christian,
virtuous and guilty?
At his door all are seekers
and he the sought.

God is without cause:
why are you looking for causes?
The sun of truth rises unbidden,
and with it sets the moon of learning.

In this halt of but a week,
to be is not to be,
and to come is to go.

And does the sun exist
for the cock to crow at?
What is it to him
whether you are there or not?
Many have come, just like you,
to his door.

You won't find your way
in this street; if there is a way,
it is on your road of sighs.
All of you are far
from the road of devotion:
you are like donkeys,
straying for months and years,
deluded by vain hopes;
sometimes you are virtuous,
sometimes you are wicked:
so you hope for yourselves, fear for yourselves;
but when your mask of wisdom and folly
at last turns white, you will see
that hope and fear are one.

When he* looked towards them,
the fear of him tore the curtain
of their pleasure, and they all
fled from him in haste.
All, except one.
—Why didn't you run away too?
—And why should I run from you,

*Omar, Companion of the Prophet. This passage refers to an occasion
when he disturbed some boys at play.

you fount of generosity?
You are no tyrant,
nor I a guilty slave!

If you know your own worth,
what need you care about
the acceptance or rejection of others?

Worship him as if you could see
him with your physical eyes;
though you don't see him,
he sees you.

Listen to the ringdove's longing cry:
two grains of barley change it into joy.

Whilst in this land
of fruitless pursuits,
you are always unbalanced, always
either all back or all front;
but once the seeking soul has progressed
just a few paces beyond this state,
loves seizes the reins.

While this world remains,
that one cannot be;
whilst you exist,
God cannot be yours.

The coming of death
is the key which unlocks

the unknown domain;
but for death, the door of true faith
would remain unopened.

Desire and excess
have put man to sleep;
when death appears,
he will awaken.

All mankind is asleep,
living in a desolate world;
the desire to trascend this
is mere habit and custom,
not religion—idle fairytales.

Stop bragging in the presence
of men of the path:
better consume yourself
like burning chaff.

If you yourself
are upside down in reality,
then your wisdom and faith
are bound to be topsy-turvy.

Stop weaving a net about yourself:
burst like a lion from the cage.

Melt yourself down in this search:
venture your life and your soul
in the path of sincerity;

strive to pass from nothingness to being,
and make yourself drunk with the wine of God.

From him forgiveness comes so fast,
it reaches us before repentance
has even taken shape on our lips.

He is your shepherd,
and you prefer the wolf;
he invites you to him,
and yet you stay unfed;
he gives you his protection,
yet you are sound asleep;
Oh, well done,
you senseless upstart fool!

He heals our nature from within,
kinder to us than we ourselves are.
A mother does not love her child
with half the love that he bestows.
His kindness makes the worthless worthy;
and in return he is content
with his servants' gratitude and patience.

You have broken faith,
yet still he keeps his faith with you:
he is truer to you
than you are to yourself.

He created your mental powers;
yet his knowledge is innocent
of the passage of thought.

He knows what is in your heart;
for he made your heart along with your clay;
but if you think that he knows
in the same way that you do,
then your are stuck like a donkey
in your own mud.

He has prior knowledge of the inmost thought;
he perceives what his creatures need
before the desire for it has been conceived.

In his presence,
silence is the gift of tongues.
You receive your life's food
from a table bare of bread.
Man does not have it in him
to desire things the like of which
have been prepared for him.

He knows the touch
of an ant's foot
moving in darkness
over a rock.
He always knows
what is in men's minds:
you would do well
to reflect on this.

If you do wrong,
there are two ways of seeing it:

either you think he doesn't know,
—and I wonder at your lack of faith—
or else you think he knows, yet still persist,
—and I wonder at your vile impertinence.
It may be true that no man knows your secrets;
but God knows them: he is not less than man;
and if he withholds his mercy from you,
surely that means he knows your heart?
Then turn away from this wrongdoing,
lest on your final day you drown
in the sea of your own shame.

Whether or not
you take his word for it,
your bread and your life
are both from his treasury.
Should your bread be in China,
the horse is saddled already
that will take you to it,
—or bring it to you
whilst you are asleep.
I tell you that your daily bread
is as certain as the day itself:
your bread is what the day brings with it.
You hold your own life in your hands
as a pledge for your food;
concern for your life is concern for your bread;
loaf follows loaf to the edge of the grave.
Hold on to this pledge, and eat your bread;
and when the pledge has passed from your hands,
then you will eat the food of life.

God never gave anyone life,
without also giving the food to sustain it;
and when your life has left your body,
you will know for certain at last
that real nourishment has reached you.

The mean live in fear
for their daily bread:
the generous never eat
yesterday's reheated leftovers.

One spark from him brings forth
a hundred thousand stars;
one drop from him
and a myriad trees spring up.
A man in fear for his daily bread
is no man at all: he is
truly less than a woman.

Your work is revealed
to no one but God;
truly, men have no power;
so pay no heed to their meddling antics.
Fix your heart on him,
and escape from sorrow and slavery;
if you can do it, discount mankind,
and take none but him for your friend.

Love's conqueror is he
whom love conquers.

Apply yourself, hand and foot,
to the search;
but when you reach the sea,
stop talking of the stream.

Slave that you are
of fame and shame,
what is enternity to you?

Myriad obstacles stand in your way;
your courage falters and fails.
All your talk is so much wordplay
as long as you remain ensnared.

You're a newcomer yet to existence:
stop talking of eternity,
when you still can't tell your head from your foot.

When he admits you to his presence
ask from him nothing other than himself.
When he has chosen you for a friend,
you have seen all that there is to see.
There's no duality in the world of love:
what's all this talk of 'you' and 'me'?
How can you fill a cup that's full already?

Bring all of yourself to his door:
bring only a part,
and you've brought nothing at all.

And when you've reached the stage
of smiles and kisses from the friend,

count his poison honey,
and his thorns a flower.

At the gate of the King
a beggar asks for bread;
but the lover desires
food for his soul.

If you are impeded
by your own inspiration,
make of it a stick
to beat yourself.
Talk less rubbish; keep your faults in view;
and leave that bone to the dogs.
Your inner qualities exalt you to great heights:
so why do you show a dog's base spirit?
The man of noble intent
enjoys the best of both worlds;
the man who is mean like a dog,
like a dog chases from meal to meal.

While your essence is still tainted with existence,
the Kaaba is a tavern, for all your service;
but once your soul has parted from existence,
even a pagan shrine is God's abode.

Tavern-crawling wretch!
You son of a donkey!
Your understanding is muddied
by self and existence;
it is blind to that other
eternal world.

It's your own self
defining faith and unbelief:
inevitably it colours your perception.
Eternity knows nothing
of belief or unbelief;
for a pure nature
there is no such thing.

And if, my friend, you ask me the way,
I'll tell you plainly, it is this:
to turn your face toward the world of life,
and turn your back on rank and reputation;
and, spurning outward prosperity, to bend
your back double in his service;
to part company with those who deal in words,
and take your place in the presence of the wordless.

When Bayazid said, 'Glory unto me!'
he did not speak in ignorance or folly;
and the tongue that uttered that final secret
moved truly when announcing, 'I am God'.
When Mansur tried to teach the back
the secret that the face had taught him,
it turned hangman and destroyed him;
his secret's daylight then became pitch darkness.
Yet it was God's own word that he spoke;
and when in the crowd he suddenly disclosed
the forbidden secret, his outer form
was given to the gallows; but the friend
took his inner being to himself;
and when his life could speak no more,

his heart's blood still disclosed the secret.

The way is not far
from you to the friend:
you yourself are that way:
so set out along it.

You who know nothing of the life
that comes from the juice of the grape,
how long will you remain intoxicated
by the outward form of the grape?
Why do you lie that you are drunk?

If you drink wine, keep quiet about it:
a milk-drinker says nothing, so why should you?
Whenever you drink a cup of wine
in this ruined house, take my advice:
don't step outside the door of your drunkenness,
but lay your head down where you have drunk;
drink in concealment, and when you have drunk,
rub soil in your lips; and not until
you've twice drunk wine and headache to the lees,
will I say of you, 'There goes a man!'

How can you go forward?
There is no place to go;
how will you leap?
You have no foot.

It is not just today
that the non-existent have come to serve

at the door of true being;
since time began, bereft of wealth and power,
servants have swarmed like ants
to wait at love's door.

Arrange things so that when death calls,
he finds your soul waiting in the street.
Leave this house of vagabonds:
if you are at God's door, stay there;
if not, make your way there now.

No one knows how far it is
from nothingness to God.
As long as you cling to your self
you will wander right and left,
day and night, for thousands of years;
and when, after all that effort,
you finally open your eyes,
you will see your self, through inherent defects,
wandering round itself like the ox in a mill;
but, if, once freed from your self,
you finally get down to work,
this door will open to you within two minutes.

God will not be yours,
as long as you cling to soul and life:
you cannot have both this and that.
Bruise your self for months and years on end;
leave it for dead, and when you have done with it,
you will have reached eternal life.

Remain unmoved by hope and fear.
To non-existence mosque and church are one;
to a shadow, heaven and hell likewise.
For someone whose guide is love,
belief and disbelief are equally a veil,
concealing the doorway of the friend;
—his very being is a veil
which hides God's essence.

Leave behind your hypocrisy
when you step into his presence.
Men of the path walk in trust;
if your trust in him is constant,
trust also in his feeding you.

It's easy to waken a sleeping man;
but the heedless are as good as dead.

How long will you talk
of trusting in God,
and call yourself man,
when you're less than a woman?
Since you cannot behave
like a man on this journey,
go and learn how from women.
Alas for the man
who is less than a woman!

The head has two ears;
love has just one:
this hears certitude,
whilst those hear doubt.

Until you throw your sword away,
you'll not become a shield;
until you lay your crown aside,
you'll not be fit to lead.

The death of soul
is the destruction of life;
but death of life
is the soul's salvation.

Never stand still on the path:
become non-existent; non-existent even
to the notion of becoming non-existent.
And when you have abandoned both
individuality and understanding,
this world will become that.

Up now, pass this world of baseness by,
and find your way to the ineffable;
pass life and body, faith and reason by,
and on the road to God acquire a soul.

Just as your outward form conceals your attributes,
your attributes dam up your inmost essence.
Form and attributes are the niche and glass
from which the light of essence shines.

Till you have endured dire straits on that road,
your soul is two-faced, though your form is one.

Tell me this—
if you are not dead or sleeping—

tell me from your fund of knowledge
of philosophy and law:
since you are endowed with a soul,
what more could you want
in exchange for your self?

You can't tell the difference
between that hidden world and this,
between well-being and suffering.
Truly you're not a man
on this path:
you're nothing but a boy;
—get back to your games,
your pride and independence,
your girlfriend's airs and graces,
since that's what pleases you.
My son,
what have you and God in common?
you reject the future
for what is here:
what can you know of eternity?
He knows how base you are:
how should he invite your self to his?
He offers you eternal joy and beauty,
yet you remain enthralled
by the beauties of this present world.
My futile friend, try to be more
than a feeble boy on the path to God.

Go to school for a while with the prophets:
abandon this madness, this sickness;

read just one page of the prophets' teaching;
since you know nothing of what they say,
go, read and learn; perhaps you'll befriend them,
perhaps you'll escape all this foolishness;
and don't imagine in this world of deceit
there is anything worse than foolishness.

If you wish for a pearl
you must leave the desert
and wander by the sea;
and even if you never find
the gleaming pearl, at least
you won't have failed to reach the water.

The man who disowns
the earth and water
of his existence
rides on the air like fire.

Whatever you own,
abandon it for the sake of God;
for charity is the greater marvel
when it comes from beggars.

Nothing in the world
can harm you like prosperity;
no prison in the world
binds like the prison of existence.

Abandon talk,
say goodbye to your lower self;

and if you cannot, let your eyes
flow like rivers, day and night,
in sorrow at your separation from God.
Grieve over your understanding;
stop using it for evil purposes.
Freed from this tether,
you will find your task easy.
And when you taste the soul's nourishment
you will survey your surroundings
from the window of the angel world.

Lower yourself in submission,
and become the beloved
of every dwelling.

When the eye is pure
it sees purity.

The vain and headstrong
are abject, dust-blown beggars;
but those he crowns are kings indeed.

Throw off that multicoloured
cloak of deceit;
take, like Jesus,
to a coat of one colour.

Unself yourself . . .
until you see your self as a speck of dust
you cannot possibly reach that place;
self could never breathe that air,
so wend your way there without self.

The Old Man of Basra

'I get up each morning,
intent on escaping this vile self.
It says to me, "Come on, old man,
what do you want to eat this morning?
Come on, get moving, what am I to eat?"
I answer "Death". and leave the subject.
Than my self says to me "What shall I wear?"
And I reply, "A winding sheet."
Then: "Where do you wish to go today?"
"Be quiet!" I say. "I'll go to the graveside,
and maybe there, at odds with my own self,
I'll draw a breath in freedom from my fear".'

In three prisons,
deceit, hatred and envy,
you are your body's captive;
your five senses
are prison spies and trusties.
In this country
the soul is a stranger,
—and a fool at that,
as long as it remains
ensnared by the senses.
How can a soul,
knowing what it knows,
keep company with spies and slanderers?

His is the tongue of the dumb.
The unmarked seek some mark of him.
Throw all but the friend into the fire;

37

on the journey from this life to the next,
we have no accomplice in good or evil;
do not give way to your heart's desire
for the society of men:
cut yourself off from them,
before they cut your throat.
On the last day you will grow tired of men;
but now you are far off, and the way is long.
What price then your diet of stinking onions,
when entry is denied you on the straight path?
Those who are not friends of yours,
although now you take them to be such,
you will see them all break faith with you.
The garden roses of the self-cherishers
will then assume the form of malignant boils.

Be clear about this: at the last day
a man's condition will be unaltered:
whatever he chooses will be set before him;
he will see there what he takes from here.

The weavers of the eternal world
will read your poetry back to you.
Whatever the shopkeeper sends home from the market
is served up at home for him in the evening;
likewise, what you take from here is kept
and brought before you at the resurrection.
Nor is there any change or substitution:
an evil cannot turn into a good.
Nothing will be given free to anyone:
you're given what is owing—nothing else.

When will you plant your foot on heaven's roof?
and when drink wine out of the angel's cup?
Can God in kindness take you to himself,
or willingly accept your prayers,
while, like a donkey in this ruined house,
your guts are full of food and drink?
How can you ever see the lawgiver,
your bottom half in mud, your nose in heaven?

With his tail the dog sweeps out his lair,
but do you sweep with sighs your place of prayer?

Your self-esteem performs no prayers,
since it sees no profit there for you.
While self-esteem is at the helm,
I doubt if Gabriel will arrive.
When on the path you have slain your self,
you will at once be shown God's favour;
to gain admission, come in poverty:
if not, you're irrevocably divorced.

When you sincerely enter into prayer,
you will come forth with all your prayers answered;
but a hundred prayers that lack sincerity
will leave you still the bungler that you are,
your work a failure; prayers said from habit
are like the dust that scatters in the wind.
The prayers that reach God's court are uttered by
    the soul;
the mimic remains a worthless, witless beggar,

who has chosen the road to madness; on this path
prayer of the soul prevails, not barren mimicry.

You come to God in all your pride:
how shall he hear you when you call?
Let your prayer be free from self;
while tainted with self he will not hear it.
What the tongue utters in helpless anguish
is a messenger from this world to God;
when it's your helplessness sending the messenger,
your cry is 'O my God!' His: 'Here I am!'

Without right guidance
man is less than an animal;
without right guidance
man labours in vain.

Fool, make an end of this servility!
Never again accept the name of servant.
If you were mighty in the world,
you would say word for word what Pharaoh said,
who in his boundless insolence and folly,
spurning all service and submissiveness,
drew aside the veil from his actions,
and said, 'I am greater than the kings,
I am above the princes of this world.'
Everyone has this insolence and pride:
these words are second nature in all men;
but fearing to divulge their secret,
they seek to hide it even from themselves.

My friend, on the path of sincerity
you are feebler than a woman—
you lag far behind
your female fellow-creatures.
Until your prayers come from the heart,
you'll never gain your soul's release.

The bone on your plate is in itself
no delicacy without the marrow;
the marrow of prayer lies in humility:
without humility prayer will not be heard.
A man must enter into prayer
sore-wounded and in poverty;
without humility and trust,
the devil will lead him by the nose.

Free your prayers
from the breath of desire;
for the dew of desire
corrupts them utterly.
Your prayers are so worthless
that the shoes from your feet
are the only gift you bring.

And speak pleasantly
when you come to the mountain:
why do you have to bray like an ass?
In the path of prayer
you have summoned up a horde of ruffians
who drown your cries.

Faced with the command
'Be, and it was,'
who dares to question
what, how and whence?

He hears the lowly, suppliant voice
of the heart; he knows
when the heart's secret rises up to him.
When supplication opens the door of the heart,
what is desired comes forth to meet it;
The answering cry, 'Here I am!' of the friend
goes out to welcome the heart's 'O my Lord!'
rising up from the highway of submission.
Whether men do good or ill,
mercy and bounty still proceed from him.

In his court,
poverty is a treasured jewel:
you bring as your gift
worldly possessions and profit;
but it is your enduring sorrow
that he finds acceptable.

You, the life of all contented men,
who grant the desires of the desirous,
what I do right is done by you,
you who are kinder to me
than I am to myself.
There are no bounds to your mercy,
no pause in your bounty.

Whatever you give me,
give me faith;

accept and allow me
near to yourself;
gladden my heart
with the thought of divinity;
inflame this body
of dust and wind!

It is your part to hand out
forgiveness and mercy;
mine to falter and fall.
Fool that I am, take me,
stumbling drunk that I am,
take my hand.

How well I know
that you conceal me;
your concealment of me
has made me proud.

I do not know
what things eternity rejects,
or who will be summoned at the last.
I am powerless either
to vex or appease you;
nor is my praise of any use to you.

My wandering heart now
seeks to rejoin you;
my uncleanness is washed
by the tears of my eyes.

Show my straying heart the way,
open a door before my eyes;
so that I neither vaunt your capacity
nor am afraid of your self-sufficiency.

You who shepherd this flock
with your mercy . . .
But what words are these?
Shepherd, flock, mercy,
all are you.

Have mercy on my soul
and on my clay;
assuage my soul's sorrow.
Cherish me, for others are hard;
take me to yourself,
for others are torn apart.

How could I befriend other than you?
They are dead: you my sufficient friend.
But what is the sense of this duality,
—believing that I am I and you are you?
What is all this smoke beside your fire?
Since you are, let all else cease to be.
The whole of existence
is merely the wind of your favour,
you from whom pain
is better than all the wealth in the world.

What kind of a madman
could ever have enough of you?
Can a man exist or stay alive

without your help or favour?
How can one grieve, possessing you;
or, lacking you, how can one prosper?
If I possess you
I am a coin of solid gold;
but lacking you I am nothing
but the creak of a millwheel.

What you told me not to taste,
I have tasted;
What you told me not to do,
I have done.
I am in agony for fear of death;
—you be my life, so that I do not die!
Why do you send your word and sword to me?
What am I apart from you?

As long as you bestow your favour,
you who are innocent of causality,
what difference if this heap of dust
be fair or foul?
This is the dust's supreme attainment:
that it can speak in praise of you.

Faced with your decree,
even if I were wisdom itself,
yet what am I that I should count
as good or evil?
Accepted by you
my evil becomes good;
rejected by you
my good becomes evil.

Lord, everything is you, both good and bad;
and the marvel is, no evil comes from you.

Checkmated on passion's chessboard,
thirsting for the heavenly oasis,
not one of us knows good from evil:
give us what you know to be good.
You, the desire of the desirous
the hope of the hopeful,
you, who know what is hidden
and see what is manifest,
carry our hopes through to certainty.

Their heaven in the sky
is full of callow youths;
in your heaven are those
who have supped in hell.
What difference fair or foul to me,
when waiting at your door;
and what is paradise to me,
compared to your presence?

Those who love you
weep in their laughter;
those who know you
laugh in their weeping.

To burn in your fire
is paradise;
but most men settle for
mere sensual delight.

If you send me from your door to hell,
I will submit and gladly go;
and if you offer poison to my soul,
sugar will seem the bitterest thing there is.

Said one old fox to another:
'Here's two hundred pence,
now run along with a message,
from me to those dogs there.'
Said the other, 'The pay
is better than a kick in the teeth;
but it's a heavy, dangerous job;
and when I've spent my life in the venture,
what use will your money be to me then?'

God is his friend, who is no friend of self;
no man with eyes on self has eyes for God.
If you are really a man of the path
abstain awhile from looking at yourself.

Merciful and mighty Lord,
do not turn me from your door;
hold me captive, take away my sleep;
let me thirst for you alone:
do not give me mere water to drink.
Why should I search high and low for you?
This pain of mine is the very chart
that leads me to you, my destination.

Time and again
you go at your worthless life
like an unbridled donkey

with fodder in front of it.
Idly you drift
from city to city:
why don't you seek what you lost
where you lost it?
If your donkey was stolen
from you in Iraq,
what are you doing
in Yazd and Rai?

Until you are complete,
a bridge has been prepared;
but once you have become complete,
what are bridge and river to you?

Malice and rancour are unknown to him:
anger is a sign of impurity;
you cannot speak of 'the wrath of God',
for he has no such attribute;
anger and hatred stem from compulsion
and both are equally far from him.
From the creator comes nothing but mercy;
he is the veiler of his servants' sins.
His mercy counsels, his grace ensnares you;
whether you come or not, he calls;
he offers you paradise in his kindness;
but in this abode of ignorance and folly,
you have chosen the path of evasiveness.

Let others be heedless; you be prudent,
and hold your tongue along this path.

The bargain is to take your food and drink
straight from the causer, never from the causes.
If you desire love, go and suffer hardship,
or else settle for the road to hell.
No one reached his goal without suffering;
until you burn them what difference is there
between willow wood and aloes wood?

Till he suffers hardship, say the wise,
a man's cup never fills to overflowing;
living in terror, he is food for hell:
even in hell he's nothing but a stone.

As long as you seek love with selfish eyes,
the crucible of regret awaits you.
And, whoever is hot on the trail of love,
the key to the door is renunciation.
Love with the beloved is delight indeed;
craving the beloved is far from God.
Your pleasures are legion: they will consume you;
The urge to love is a caress from heaven.

When life finally walks out of the door,
your tattered soul is straight away renewed;
your form is freed from the bonds of nature,
and your soul gives back the spirit's loan.

Gabriel, forever in the heat of the chase,
bathes his face in the water of life.
Reason is unhinged by his soul's outcry;
Devils are tinder to his flashing horseshoes.

None of the patient and outwardly pious
will learn the secret of his sigh,
or find the traces of his path.
Wherever his horseshoes scatter the dust,
Gabriel leaves a life-giving fragrance.

When the sunlight falls on water,
the ripples' movement is reflected,
and throws a brilliant picture on the wall:
remember that this secondary reflection
is also from the sun.

Whether you exist or not
is indifferent to the working of God's power.
Everything is the work of God alone,
—and happy is the man that knows it!

Reason was the pen, self the paper;
matter was given form; bodies received their shapes.
To love he said 'Fear none but me'.
To reason his words were, 'Know yourself'.

Whilst you live in this residence,
this tomb allotted to you,
this home of distraction and deceit,
look upon the willow with your earthly eye,
and with your soul upon the tree of paradise.
Read the letters with your tongue,
read their meaning with your soul.

As long as your desire is pleasure,
and you cherish your desire,

carry on playing like a child:
you are not man enough for this.

You, who have brought nothing back
but foam from the ocean,
you, with your possessions
arrayed around you,
you have not grasped the essence of the pearl,
being forever engrossed in the oyster shell.
Leave these muddy shells alone;
bring up the pure pearl from the ocean depths.

The arrow's worth lies in hitting the mark.
If you are pure, the hidden sense
will emerge from the framework
of the written word;
for until a man steps out from impurity,
how can the Quran step out from the page?
As long as you are veiled in self,
how can you discriminate
between good and evil?
The letter of the Quran is in itself
no panacea for the soul:
Goats don't grow fat on the goatherd's call.

Why claim to be somebody
in this village of yours?
The only thing that singles you out
is that to be nothing at all
is better than any such distinction.
You may think you are something

but that something is nothing.
You think you amount to something?
—So do the dots on a dice!

It's a happy man who has effaced
his imprint from the world,
neither seeking nor sought by anyone.

Whoever is caught up in the bonds of this world
stands only to gain if he flees its might;
for this world is the source of pain and sorrow:
the wise have called it a transit camp.
Since in the light of reason and vision,
two timely flights are worth three victories,
it surely is the height of folly
for you to linger on this bridge.

AFTERWORD

'... why should not the translator or interpreter declare his real interest and not pass off the next as an embodiment of the real manuscript or text?'

Sheikh Hassan Effendi.*

As was stated in the foreword, these notes were gathered from Major J. Stephenson's edition, which is entitled: 'The first book of the Hadiqatu'l-Haqiqat, or the Enclosed Garden of the Truth, of the Hakim Abu'l-Majdud Sanai of Ghazna.' Perhaps I need go no further than that mouthful in order to explain what impelled me to write notes. Confronted with a title like that, anyone might be forgiven for simply blinking and then reaching for the Radio Times. And yet, when a copy of Major Stephenson's book came into my hands for a brief period in 1968, I became rapidly convinced that buried deep in this formidable tome there lay a message of great directness and power, but that in its present form there was precious little chance of that message ever reaching precisely those people who might

*As reported by Rafael Lefort in *The Teachers of Gurdjieff*, Gollancz, London 1966, p. 66.

53

derive most benefit from it. I may be wrong, and would be delighted to be proven so, but it is my deep suspicion that no more than a handful of people have ever read either the Persian or the English of Major Stephenson's edition. Frankly, it does not seem designed to be read, but rather to sit there on the shelf, yet another chilly monument to academic endeavour.

The book consists of the Persian text of the first part (i.e. about one sixth) of Sanai's *Hadiqat*, which in its entirety runs to almost 12,000 rhyming couplets, together with a copiously annotated translation in somewhat fulsome Edwardian prose. There is an introduction giving much useful background material, and a lengthy discussion of the translator's attempt—and failure—to arrive at a 'definitive' text.

It was certainly a daunting task which Major Stephenson set himself, especially since he was so obviously a scholar of the highest conscientiousness and integrity. Manuscripts of the *Hadiqat* amount to something of an orientalist's nightmare. The text, as Stephenson puts it, '. . . fell into confusion at a very early date.' He worked from five separate manuscripts, and he confesses that his initial selection was 'somewhat arbitrary'. In his book, a full twenty-nine closely-printed pages are devoted to listing the variant readings which he unearthed in his collation of the texts. In addition to the thousands of textual variations, there seemed to be no agreement among the several manuscripts as to the arrangement of sections or even individual lines of the poem (p. xxi). The Major freely admits: 'I am very far from imagining that we have

54

arrived at any close approximation to the author's original.'

Does it matter? For someone who is interested primarily in what Sanai is actually saying, the tattered fragments remain, imperfect, confused, but certainly better than nothing. I was very glad of the opportunity to read Hakim Sanai at all; and at once set about making notes of those sections of the text and translation which seemed to have the most immediate impact. Armed with these notes, I worked intermittently during the following years, producing what I hoped would be a readable—and speakable—modern English version of those selections. At first I merely confined myself to polishing and simplifying Major Stephenson's version. But later a friend was kind enough to make me an extended loan of his copy of the text; and I was able to work through the material again much more thoroughly, adding many sections which I had initially overlooked, and paying much closer attention to the original Persian.

As a result my present version has a somewhat variegated parentage. Some of it I have taken on trust from Major Stephenson and simply put into more acceptable modern English; the greater part of it I have checked through in the Persian; occasionally I have made a completely fresh translation from the original. There is also considerable variation in the closeness of my version to the original: sometimes it is a literal, word for word translation; elsewhere it is a paraphrase or occasionally even a precis of Sanai's words.

The Stephenson edition represents about one sixth of the original; and I suppose my selection comprises a similar fraction of Stephenson's material. There can therefore be no question of claiming for this version that it constitutes 'an embodiment of the real manuscript or text.' It is simply a series of disconnected notes abstracted from the text and presented in the order in which they appear in the Stephenson edition.

The temptation to shuffle these notes into a more aesthetically satisfying order was considerable; but there seemed just as much advantage in leaving them as they stood. The sudden changes and breaks in continuity, the scattering of recurring themes throughout the material may serve as a reminder that we are dealing with highly fragmented and incomplete material, and save us from being lulled into what would inevitably be an illusory sense of order and system. In any case I felt that I had done more than enough violence to the original by the very process of selection. To try now to disguise this would be to add insult to injury.

The principles which guided my selection are bound to be highly subjective. I merely recorded those passages which made an impact on me. Another interpreter might well assemble a very different set of quotations. For example, I have soft-pedalled on the traditional Moslem elements which are very much in evidence throughout the book. Much of Sanai's material caters for an audience imbued with the letter if not with the spirit of the *Quran* and the *Hadith* (sayings of Muhammed). There seemed little point in including such material for its own sake, since the conditions which necessitated its inclusion in the first place do not exist here and now. Moreover the effect would be the reverse of what was intended: designed to make Sanai's audience feel 'at home', it would simply estrange a Western reader of Christian extraction. Sanai had to present impeccable orthodox credentials in order to be allowed to introduce other materials which, though essentially of greater value, could be and were indeed regarded as heretical by the bigots of his day. It is these latter materials that I have sought to include here. In general I have avoided allusions which demand a specialized knowledge of Moslem culture, retaining only such concepts as have already gained currency in English.

To return to the withering quotation with which I began my essay, I have to admit that my version falls as far short of Sanai's in quality as it does in quantity. I cannot claim to have done more than skate over the surface of Sanai's poem. Many passages lend themselves to a number of different interpretations; and it is usually impossible to retain this ambivalence in translation—even assuming that the translator is sensitive to it in the first place. I suspect that in the hands of a Sufi specialist the most innocent, even banal, sections of the text could be made to yield up extremely subtle meanings. In my version I have not attempted to grapple with such subtleties; but the handful which I happened to notice lead me to speculate that there must be literally hundreds of others which escaped my attention. A single example will have to suffice.

In the couplet following the one rendered here as:

> 'I was a hidden treasure;
> creation was created
> so that you might know me.'

Sanai continues: 'From (the arabic letters) *Kaf* and *Nun*,
like a precious pearl, he made the eye into a mouth
filled with (the arabic letters) *Ya Sin*'. *Kaf* and *Nun* are
the letters of the arabic word *Kun*—God's primordial
command: 'Be!' The letters *Ya Sin* are the cryptic
initials which head *sura* 36 of the Quran. Major
Stephenson and the annotators of the manuscripts he
uses have had a field-day trying to make sense out of
this couplet, as have commentators of the Quran
discussing the significance of the initials *Ya Sin*. The
latter generally come to the same conclusion as Abdulla
Yusuf Ali, that '. . . no dogmatic assertion can be made
about the abbreviated letters.' Be that as it may, Sanai
in this couplet is clearly indicating an association
between the letters YS and the letters KN. If we now
apply the '*abjad*' formula (whereby Arabic words may be
given numerical values and then recoded into other
words) we arrive at the following:

$$Y = 10; S = 60; \qquad 10 + 60 = 70.$$
$$K = 20; N = 50; \qquad 20 + 50 = 70.$$

It is a fairly safe assumption that Sanai is thus intending
to signal the numerical equivalence of KN with YS.
And, turning to the *Ya Sin Sura* (36) in the Quran, we
find in the last verse but one the stirring divine command: '*Kun fayakun*!'—'Be, and it was!'

If we return now to Sanai's couplet, what we might
forgivably have regarded as little more than gibberish

is suddenly pregnant with meaning. One line of interpretation might be this: the 'eye' is the visionary basis and the 'mouth' is the expression in words of the Quran. Or, on a broader scale, the 'eye' is divine consciousness and the mouth is the manifestation of that consciousness in creation. The essential link lies in the command, '*Kun!*', which embodies in a way unparalleled in the literature of the world the notion of conscious creativity. One is immediately reminded of the opening phrase of St. John's gospel: 'In the beginning was the Word . . .'. But the Quran goes further, and ventures to tell us what that 'word' was. *Kun fayakun* celebrates the fundamental mystery of being, which man may ponder but never comprehend. As Gustav Fechner put it, 'Among all existing miracles the greatest is that anything should exist at all'.

The 'mouth filled with *Ya Sin*' represents the expression in all its splendour of the divine consciousness-creativity. *Sura* (36) (*Ya Sin*) is commonly characterised as 'the heart of the Quran'; and in his couplet Sanai is telling us exactly why. If *Ya Sin* is the heart, then *Kun*, the 'precious pearl', is the heart of the heart.

Sanai is thus indicating the relationship between the spirit and the letter of the Quran—a theme to which he constantly returns—and incidentally echoing that relationship in the very technique he applies. All this in the space of a single couplet, which as we now see, far from being an obscure irrelevancy, is closely connected with the preceding lines.

Of course, to subject the whole of Sanai's poem to verbal analysis of this sort would be to defeat the whole purpose of writing the poem in the first place. Such insights, if they occur at all, are instantaneous and do not need to be verbalised further; and if they do not occur then it is probably better to let them lie dormant until such time as a flash of insight is possible. My purpose here was simply to indicate that there exist dimensions in the poem to which no translator could hope to do justice.

There are many other devices of language in the *Hadiqat* which I have not attempted to convey in my version. The Persian language is suited to rhyming in a way that modern English simply is not. '*Rime riche*' is fairly standard throughout the poem; very frequently the rhymes are several words deep:

> Bar dar-e-shah gada-i nan khahad:
> baz 'asheq ghaza-ye-jan khahad.

It would be virtually impossible to produce similar rhyming patterns in English; and even if one were to try, the effect would certainly be the reverse of that obtained in Persian. We have to accept that in modern English rhyming has largely been relegated to Tin Pan Alley and Madison Avenue.

And yet a strict prose translation, such as Major Stephenson's, represents a sorry dilution of the original impact in Persian. I have therefore opted for a variety of very loose verse forms, which amount to little more than a stabilization of certain inherent rhythmic patterns in our language. In this way I hope at least to remind the reader of the poetic origins of the work. And for the same reason, whenever I have unconsciously

chanced on a rhyme in my version, I have deliberate
retained it—in memory of more poetic times.

As with rhyming, so with the many other forms of
word-play in which Hakim Sanai continually indulges.
Arabic, and the Arabized languages of the Middle East
are extremely sensitive to homophones and to multiple
meanings of the same word. So serious is the status
awarded to juggling with words and their meanings,
that 'wordplay' is hardly the correct description of it. In
English we have the 'pun'—a form of speech in which
Shakespeare himself took great delight; but at its best
it was never more than a witty seasoning to language;
and nowadays it has come to be seen as a mark of
puerile humour. Yet such devices abound in almost
every line of Sanai's verse: they are almost as integral
to it as alliteration is to Anglo-Saxon. The intention,
however, is seldom humorous, but rather to underline
the point he is making and to fix it in the mind of his
audience. Here is one example:

> Pish-e-*shar*'at zi *shar* jastan beh:
> *bait*-ra humchu *but* shikastan beh.

This may be rendered as:
> According to your *religion* (shar')
> it is better to shun *poetry* (shar')
> —to shatter your *verse* (bait)
> as you would an *idol*. (but)

Not infrequently a sound effect is produced which is
strikingly reminiscent of such gems of pre-adolescent
wordplay as:

61

Q. What's the difference between a mad circus-
owner and a Roman Barber?

A. One is a shaving Roman and the other's a raving
showman.

But as in the previous example Sanai's intention is
emphasis, not humour.

This is perhaps a good moment to question the somewhat facile assumption that because in our culture the
fascination of secret codes, rhyming, punning, spooner-
isms, etc., tends to wane with the onset of puberty, such
activities are inherently childish and immature. Indeed
when we find a culture, like Sanai's, in which these
preoccupations persist, in correspondingly more so-
phisticated forms, right into adult life, we may even
begin to wonder why this capacity seems to atrophy so
soon in the West. Far from having outgrown an
infantile mode of behaviour, it may be argued that we
have failed to develop its potential adult stage—a very
valuable counterweight to the hypnotic power of linear
verbal communication. Naturally our thinkers write and
speak words—and yet everything is ruthlessly excluded
from their communications which might serve to remind us that what is actually being communicated is not
thought, but mere words. Language has become for us
like water: a tasteless, odourless, colourless medium;
and like fish we only are aware of its existence when for
some reason we are suddenly deprived of it. We are
effectively anaesthetized to words; and perhaps
precisely for that very reason we have been more en-
slaved by them than any other culture in history. It is
salutory to observe communities where even the

simplest people seem capable of maintaining a certain ironic detachment from what they say and hear; where it is not immediately assumed that the broadcast or printed word should carry more weight than the spoken word, or the spoken more than the unspoken.

The reader may be beginning to wonder what, if anything, remains of Sanai's poem in the present version; but I have yet to mention the greatest flaw; it does not lie in academic or technical incompetence—considerable though these are—but in the relationship in which the present writer finds himself to what Sanai is teaching. Rebellious and confused, I hesitate at the outset of a journey which the Sage of Ghazna has already completed. Seeing the impertinence of selecting and interpreting his teaching in my own words has more than once prompted me to scrap the whole venture as an outrageous piece of vanity. Two things enabled me to see the task through to some sort of conclusion.

Firstly I have to thank the encouragement of friends, who were too sincere to pretend that such misgivings were illusory, but at the same time reminded me that 'a good painting can sometimes come from a bad brush'; that there is no vanity like concealing vanity.

Secondly there was the bond of affection and gratitude which slowly developed in the course of contact with Sanai and what he represents. I felt that he was addressing me, and those like me, in a spirit of total sincerity; and that listening to him and actively trying to assimilate what he was saying lent a kind of stability to the superficial turmoil and folly of life.

A more scathing and unsparing teacher one could

hardly imagine, who unceasingly showers his audience with a stream of highly unflattering epithets—'senseless, upstart fool', 'son of a donkey', 'tavern-crawling wretch', and so on; but to be offended by such blunt accusations of folly and ignorance is somehow to lend them added justification. They are not made in order to reduce us to a state of snivelling penitence, but rather to shock us out of that unhealthy craving for flattery and approval which we habitually and unthinkingly expect writers to satisfy. They are not made in a spirit of malice and contempt, but come from the lips of some-one who has seen all these weaknesses all too clearly in *himself*, and has succeeded in escaping beyond them; someone who is able to discern such weaknesses in others, and point them out in such a way that even his most virulent castigations of man's perverse stupidity are imbued with the affirmation that there does indeed exist a nobler condition, more worthy of human beings. Reading Sanai, one can indeed 'count his poison honey'.

What has passed for 'spiritual' teaching among us has generally tended to come in one of two forms. Either it consists of syrupy reassurances that 'God's in his heaven all's right with the world'; or else it comes within the same category as the Wesleyan hellfire sermon. Of course, neither approach is 'spiritual' in any meaningful sense of the term, being no more than a thinly dis-guised appeal to the emotions of hope and fear within us all.

Saturated as we are by these forms of communication, we are ill-prepared for Sanai's approach, which cuts completely across this polarity. For a perception of the true situation, both actual and potential, hope and fear are equally useless. In Hakim Sanai's view man is neither good nor evil: he is merely ignorant and stupid; and until he can recognize this, he bars himself from any possibility of progress. Such dual concepts as good and evil, faith and unbelief, heaven and hell etc., are our greatest stumbling blocks. Sanai's intention is neither to woo nor to scare us into some kind of momentous emotional upheaval which in our vanity we will then misrepresent to ourselves and others as a religious 'conversion'. Rather he seeks little by little to erode that vanity, so that more positive qualities may have room to develop.

The prime target of Sanai's onslaught is the 'self' (*nafs*). By this term he understands something like the 'ego' of western psychology: the provisional 'consensus-reality' which we passively allow environment, culture and experience to erect around us from birth. The self is an entirely illusory entity, constantly changing, full of contradictions which only habit prevents us from discerning. But above all the self is—selfish. As if flying in panic from any recognition of its own nothingness, it feverishly erects edifices of self-importance, self-aggrandizement, self-love. More binding than any prison, since we unthinkingly take its very walls for reality, it prevents us from ever realizing the true significance of our being here.

The self is a fiction; beyond it, asserts Sanai, lies the reality of God (*haqq*). The process of disentanglement from self is the first step on the path to that reality;

and that first step, he continually reminds, us, is the all-important one.

Reality is a synonym for God in Muslim thought. Both Jesus and the Muslim martyr Mansur al Hallaj figure prominently in Sanai's poem as exemplars of total identification with that reality to the complete exclusion of self. Many striking parallels in the roles adopted by Jesus and Mansur are readily apparent to anyone not committed to the belief that Jesus is entirely beyond comparison with other men.* At all events, both are said to have uttered the same ostensibly blasphemous proclamation, 'I am the truth', and as a result to have suffered death at the hands of an outraged community.

Mansur's utterance (*ana'l haqq*) was taken by contemporaries to be the supreme blasphemy and arrogance. Only God was entitled to such an attribute. What was meant, however, was the very reverse of arrogant: that the self had been annihilated and only God remained. Speaking of such pronouncements in his *Memoirs of the Saints*, Attar says: 'It is God who is speaking through them. Their self is dead.'†

For Sanai, then, the self is unreality and God the reality. He is also The Friend. To divest oneself of self is a gain, not a loss; it is far from plunging into 'the eternal silence of those infinite spaces', which so terrified Blaise Pascal. God, as apprehended by Sanai, is the very reverse of remote and unapproachable. He is

Anthology of Islamic Literature, Ed. J. Kritzeck (Pelican, London, 1964 pp. 104–113.)
†Fariduddin Attar: *Tadhkaratul-Auliya*, (Ashraf Press, Lahore, 1961) p. 141.

66

approached as one would a beloved friend. One of the most striking features of Sanai's poetry—and indeed almost all Sufi poetry—is the way in which a complete analogy is drawn between the ideals of human love and divine love. A human love worthy of the name is one in which the participants transcend the self, in which the sense of 'I' and 'you' is completely left behind in the fulness of the supervening contact. To experience this, however fleetingly, is to have an intimation of the reality of God.

Sufism has always recognized this capacity as the fulcrum of human evolution, and has developed a massive repertoire of methods designed to activate the full potential of what generally remains a gratuitous, perhaps once-in-a-lifetime experience. Central in this activity is the figure of the teacher. The special form of friendship and love which grows between teacher and pupil is simultaneously a bond of friendship between man and God. Such a process is the very reverse of hero-worship. The teacher systematically and very effectively rejects those manifestations from his charges which have their origins in the self. Pupils are weaned at the outset from the tendency to fixate and identify with authority figures. If this first lesson is not learnt, there are no others. The teacher is merely a channel of communication; his presence may elicit love and devotion from those around him, but these are destined not for himself but for the reality his teaching represents: 'The teacher's acceptance is the nearest thing to divine acceptance and represents it as far as it can'.* He is able to transmit

*Idries Shah: *The Sufis*, (W. H. Allen, London, 1964) p. 266.

this 'divine acceptance' for the sufficient reason that his motives have, by virtue of his own training, been divested of self, and are entirely at the disposal of a higher purpose. There is no arrogance in the claim that the true teacher-pupil relationship is an exact counterpart of God's relationship with mankind. It is a simple technical fact which does no particular credit to either participant. When Sufis are accused, as they so often have been, of 'worshipping' their teachers, the accusation merely reveals a pessimistic under-valuation of the potential latent in human friendship, and a very primitive understanding of the kind of relationship that exists between man and God.

In the light of these remarks a striking ambivalence may be discerned in Sanai's poem. So far we have taken it at face value, as a treatment of man's quest for God; but the same words can be made to serve equally well as an illustration of the relationship of the seeker to his guide. Seen in this light, the poem takes on a much more practical aspect.

In the present mood of our culture one senses that some kind of apology is called for whenever the word 'God' is introduced. The trend in the West is for us to become bigots in reverse—to reject blindly and vehemently what our ancestors with equal blindness and vehemence used to affirm. What is remarkable is that Sanai's message has an equal relevance in either climate.

Who has not taken part *ad nauseam* in futile, never-ending debates on the issue of the existence of God? The discussion always seems to polarize a particular group into two factions. One side expect to be presented with some kind of Pythagorean demonstration, and when it is not forthcoming, complacently reject the whole question. The other side clench their fists around emptiness and doggedly insist that there is something in their hands for the sovereign reason that they *believe* that there is, thus making a virtue out of their blind obstinacy. The mixture may vary from culture to culture; but the overall effect remains the same. The approach implicit in the question, 'Does God exist?' is altogether inept—like trying to build a house from the roof downwards. Sanai dwells at considerable length on the pathetic irrelevance of such after-dinner metaphysics; again and again he brings us up short with: what do *you* know about it?

It is useless quibbling over a mere word, even if that word is God. To accept or reject it, when we have no knowledge of what it may represent, is equally inappropriate. God is a mystery; and the mystery remains, whatever name we give to it. He is the question, 'Who?' long before he can become the affirmation, '*Hu!*' The fact that we can pose a question does not in itself presuppose an immediate answer.

If Sanai's use of the word God offends or perplexes the reader, then perhaps he should follow up the suggestion that the poem may also be read as a description of the seeker-guide relationship; and if even that is offensive to him, he might try, before turning his back on the subject, to ask himself why he should find it so offensive. We are not discussing the guru-superstar industry. By definition the teacher has no need of gratitude and praise: if anything, they are a burden placed on him. It is the seeker who needs the experience of true gratitude, in order that he may eventually grow to understand what the real source of all his blessings is.

Hakim Sanai's influence is clearly discernible in the writings of a number of Sufi poets whose names are much more familiar in the West. Many of Sanai's ideas are re-echoed in the verse of Attar and Rumi. The famous parable of the Elephant in the Dark, best known in Rumi's version, is also to be found in Sanai's *Hadiqat*.* The striking notion, that the very act of heart-felt supplication is in itself simultaneously God's gesture of acceptance—which occurs more than once in Sanai's poem:

'When it's your helplessness sending the messenger,
    Your cry is 'O my God!' His: 'Here I am!'
and:

    'The answering cry, 'Here I am!' of the friend
    Goes out to welcome the heart's 'O my Lord!'
—appears again almost word for word in Rumi's *Masnavi*:

'Your cry of "Allah" (God says) is in itself My "Here am I"; . . . Under each "Allah" of yours whispers many a "Here am I".'†

To compile a list of such obvious parallels would be a long and ultimately pointless task. Any suggestion of 'plagiarism' is totally irrelevant. Sanai, Rumi and Attar, were all merely drawing from a single source; in such a

*Idries Shah, *Tales of the Dervishes*, Cape, London, 1967 p. 25.
†A. J. Arberry: *Tales from the Masnavi*, Allen and Unwin, London, 1961, p. 186.

situation, such notions as 'copyright' and 'precedence' are ludicrously out of place. Besides, Jalaluddin Rumi explicitly records his debt of gratitude to Sanai in the most generous terms:

'I left off boiling while still half-cooked.

Hear the full acount from the Saga of Ghazna.'

and:

'Attar was the spirit, Sanai the eyes;

we walk in the wake of Sanai and Attar.'

Such acclaim was evidently wasted on Professor Browne,* who compares Sanai most unfavourably with Mevlana Jelaluddin Rumi:

'The poem is written in a halting, unattractive metre, and is in my opinion one of the dullest books in Persian, seldom rising to the level of Martin Tupper's *Proverbial Philosophy*, filled with fatuous truisms and pointless anecdotes, and as far inferior to the Mathnavi of Jalalu'd-Din Rumi as is Robert Montgomery's *Satan* to *Paradise Lost*'.

Perhaps a more constructive appraisal is to be found in the *Miratu'l Hadaiq* of Abdu'llatif:

'In short, in sobriety Hakim is preeminent and in intoxication Mevlana is superior.'

'Sobriety' and 'intoxication' are of course not intended literally; nor are they merely flowery metaphors: these are technical terms denoting twin poles of human awareness, each in its own way indispensible to balanced development. A man has to see the true reality of his situation; he has to take a very sober look at himself. Equally, though, he needs a taste of another con-

Literary History of Persia, vol. 2, p. 319.

dition in which his latent possibilities are realized. Taken on its own, either pole is sterile, developmentally speaking. There are plentiful examples all around us of such imbalances. Perhaps you too had a Calvinist great-uncle who died heartbroken, having succeeded in convincing himself, *a.* that 'the grace of God' was essential, and *b.* that such 'grace' had been withheld from him. Perhaps you, too, have friends whose Ouspensky-orientated understanding of Gurdjieff has left eternally bewailing the (obvious) facts that 'man is asleep', 'man cannot remember himself', 'man cannot *do*', etc. Or other friends who have chosen to 'freak out', to 'blow their minds'; and are astonished, in rare moments of lucidity, to find themselves inhabiting a 'behavioural sink' or 'terminal sewer'. Or other friends, perhaps, who inform you in and out of season that: 'I was hopelessly at sea, until ... (name and address supplied) showed me the answer.'

Just as the experience of love and friendship is enlisted to provide a bridge to an understanding of man's relationship to God, in the same way the imagery of wine hints at alternative forms of consciousness beyond the so-called normal waking state. Both Sanai and Rumi endeavour to encompass both conditions in their writings, but with the differing emphasis that Abdu'llatif so rightly indicates. To say that one approach is better than the other is rather like saying that North is better than South. What is important is that the individual should find his own particular orientation, and learn to correct his own imbalance by exposure to contrary influences. If he is an 'inebriation mystic', then Sanai is there to pull him up short; if his nature is too austere, then an appropriate corrective might be found in Rumi's approach.

So much confusion has arisen in the academic study of different strands of Sufi teaching from the failure to recognize the overriding importance of the individual's situation—the specific needs of particular times, places and people. In the absence of such criteria, our literary critics are thrown back on to conventional considerations of 'entertainment value', which must inevitably be historically and geographically parochial.

Jalaluddin Rumi's work has tended to exert a rather spurious attraction by virtue of the splendours he has managed to capture in the written word. Despite his clear warnings in *Fihi ma Fihi* that in comparison with real experience, his poetry was just so much 'tripe', a following has built up around his work which stops short at the 'sublime' experience of his poetry, without ever paying the price of entry into the reality it mirrors. Rumi's comments on Sanai may be taken at face value: 'I left off cooking'—may be taken as meaning: 'I pulled my punches' (and settled for entertainment) where the Sage of Ghazna did not. That the 'full story' is found in Sanai, means that there the human condition, the starting point, is spelled out for us mercilessly and without allegory. Sanai's verse may be a tent in comparison with Rumi's palace; but when one has no shelter at all the distinction has little meaning; and a real tent is of more value than an imaginary palace—which is all that Rumi's verse has become for so many of his enthusiasts.

Sanai uses the wine allegory sparingly—but he uses

it. With him the emphasis is more on integrating 'drunkenness' (ecstasy) into everyday experience. In a milieu where it is almost as easy to obtain L.S.D. as it is to buy an ice-cream, this is perhaps the most useful aspect to emphasise: the necessity of a proper grounding in self-knowledge, rather than launching into experiences which, being incommensurate with 'consensual reality', merely render it more unworkable than it was before, without providing any practical alternative. This, then, is the meaning of Sanai's sobriety. In the words of one contemporary Sufi source:

'There are different ways of 'awakening'. Man may be asleep, but he must wake in the right way. One necessity is that when he is awake, he will also have the means to profit by his wakefulness. It is the preparation for this profiting as well as the preparation for waking, which is our current endeavour.'

READING LIST

Some Sufi Classics:

Hafiz: The Divan, Translated by Col. W. Clarke and Mirza Bisravi, London, 1974.

Rumi: The Masnavi, Translated and Abridged by E. H. Whinfield, London, 1974.

Shabistari: The Secret Garden, Translated by Johnson Pasha, London, 1969.

Travels and Residence among Sufis:

Lefort, Rafael: *The Teachers of Gurdjieff*, London, 1966.

Davidson, R. W.: *Documents on Contemporary Dervish Communities*, London, 1966.

Burke, O. M.: *Among the Dervishes*, London, 1973.

Contemporary Studies on Sufis and Sufism:

Lewin, L. (Editor): *The Diffusion of Sufi Ideas in the West*

Shah, Idries: *The Sufis*, London & New York, 1964.

Rushbrook Williams, Professor L. F., (Editor) *Sufi Studies: East and West*, New York, 1973.

Foster, W.: *Sufi Studies Today*, London, 1968.

THE SPIRIT OF THE EAST

Today the kinship of all religious thought and dogma is becoming more apparent to mankind—and the value of Oriental thought to the Occidental mind is obvious. Here is a selection from Moslem, Parsee, Hindu, Hebrew, Confucian and other sources, chosen not only for their spiritual worth but also for the particular virtues of each creed which they represent.

The aim of this book is to introduce readers to the religious thought of the East, which—for reasons of language and other difficulties—they might otherwise have considered inaccessible.

The Spirit of the East
Sirdar Ikbal Ali Shah

REFLECTIONS

This selection of Idries Shah's own fables, aphorisms and teachings is now in its fifth edition and continues to be extremely popular.

Pocket-sized, it is immensely entertaining and at the same time offers an alternative view of our society that is both refreshing and profitable.

'More wisdom than I have found in any other book this year'.   Pat Williams *Review of the Year*, BBC.

'It seems to oblige the mind to scorn the satisfaction of going from A to B in favour of an approach from a different angle, taking in unsuspected territory, hatched out as modified behaviour'.   *The Evening News.*

Reflections
by Idries Shah

TEACHINGS OF RUMI
THE MASNAVI

Jalaluddin Rumi's great work, *The Masnavi*, was 43 years in the writing. During the past seven hundred years, this book, called by Iranians 'The Koran in Persian', a tribute paid to no other book, has occupied a central place in Sufism.

'*The Masnavi* is full of profound mysteries, and a most important book in the study of Sufism—mysteries which must, for the most part, be left to the discernment of the reader.'

F. Hadland Davis

'To the Sufi, if not to anyone else, this book speaks from a different dimension, yet a dimension which is in a way within his deepest self'.

Idries Shah

'The greatest mystical poet of any age'.

Professor R. A. Nicolson

'It can well be argued that he is the supreme mystical poet of all mankind'.

Professor A. J. Arberry

Teachings of Rumi: The Masnavi
Abridged and translated by E. H. Whinfield.

SPECIAL PROBLEMS IN THE STUDY OF SUFI IDEAS

This important monograph constitutes the whole text of Idries Shah's Seminar at Sussex University, fully annotated, indexed and with a bibliography and notes.

It knits together the available knowledge about Sufi thought and literature in its passage through many deforming influences, such as the development of cults, the mis-interpretation by literalist scholars, and the fallacious comparisons of committed 'specialists'.

'Masterful essay . . . he has ably presented Sufism to the West and has conveyed its deep sense of reality to modern man . . .'

Professor A. Reza Arasteh,
Psychology of the Sufi Way

Special Problems in the Study of Sufi Ideas
by Idries Shah